ESTES PARK
Beginnings

By Kenneth Jessen

J. V. Publications L.L.C.

Estes Park Beginnings

By Kenneth Jessen
Copyright © 2011 by Kenneth Jessen

Published by J.V. Publications L.L.C., 2212 Flora Court, Loveland, CO 80537

First Edition

1 2 3 4 5 6 7 8 9

Library of Congress Control Number: 2010916792
ISBN: 978-1-928656-08-1

Printed in Canada

Cover Design: LaVonne Ewing
Interior Design: Diane Streb
Front and back cover photos by Fred Payne Clatworthy and
   hand-colored by Cheryl Pennington
Copy Editors: Sarah Holdt and Mary Edelmaier

This book is dedicated to James H. Pickering, Historian Laureate for the Town of Estes Park for his individual contributions in preserving Estes Park history through diligent, meticulous research combined with his command of the English language enabling him to communicate history with great clarity.

TABLE OF CONTENTS

INTRODUCTION

The Estes valley was visited by paleo–Indians about 12,000 years ago, but the first permanent settler was the venturesome Joel Estes, who arrived in the area in 1860 with his wife and 13 children in tow. Six years later, after trying to make a living ranching and harvesting wild game, the Estes family left the valley for a more secure and familiar existence on the plains. Other adventurers took their place in the valley, also attempting to make a livelihood from raising cattle. Yet persistent visitors, drawn to the area's incredible scenery, were knocking on the doors of these homesteaders, asking for permission to camp and wanting to purchase food. Ranchers responded by offering a few rental tents and cabins, and soon began constructing lodges to accommodate the influx of tourists. By and by, visitors demanded more time and attention than the cattle, and tourism replaced ranching as Estes Park's primary economy. An expanding community emerged, including a post office, school and several stores. A tourism town was born. Today, Estes Park is the gateway to Rocky Mountain National Park, where 3 million people visit each year.

Where the Estes Park village is located today was the property of pioneer John Cleave. In 1905, after living in the valley for 30 years, he sold his property to a town company. The village was platted, a street system was established and lots were put up for sale. A decade later, Rocky Mountain National Park was created solidifying Estes Park's position as a regional tourist center. By 1919, the entire village was almost fully developed. Recent changes in the makeup of the Town of Estes Park have come in the form of permanent rather than seasonal residents.

Kenneth Jessen
Loveland, Colorado 2011

ACKNOWLEDGMENTS

Many individuals made this book possible including Derek Fortini, Manager of the Estes Park Museum, who went through the entire collection of historic photographs and developed a valuable timeline of major events leading up to the creation of Estes Park. John Meissner provided help in dating photographs through his meticulous research into the sequence of the construction of buildings. Jim Pickering answered many questions about early businesses and clarified the sequence of events leading to the creation of the town. Bobbie Heisterkamp generously opened up her extensive collection of Estes Park postcards to help pinpoint certain dates. Cheryl Pennington set up a meeting with the daughter of Fred Payne Clatworthy, Barbra Clatworthy Gish, and in addition, Pennington hand-colored one of Clatworthy's photographs for use as the cover. Many thanks go to Mary Edelmaier and to Sarah Holdt for their talent in copy editing the manuscript and Diane Streb for her book design. Will Citta came up with the book's title.

ABOUT THE AUTHOR

This is Kenneth Jessen's nineteenth book. Selected titles include:

Railroads of Northern Colorado

Thompson Valley Tales

Eccentric Colorado

Bizarre Colorado

Colorado's Strangest

Georgetown – A Quick History

Estes Park – A Quick History

The Great Western Railway

Out the Back and Down the Path

Colorado Gunsmoke

Ghost Towns, Colorado Style volumes one, two and three

Ghost Towns, Eastern Colorado

Rocky Mountain National Park Pictorial History

plus several other titles

Jessen's articles appear twice a week in the Loveland *Reporter-Herald* and to date, he has had over 1, 300 illustrated articles published. Jessen, a tour guide and lecturer, runs a small publishing company specializing in Colorado history. Jessen and his wife, Sonje, are travelers having visited all of the continents and a third of the world's countries. They live in Loveland, Colorado and have three sons and five grandchildren.

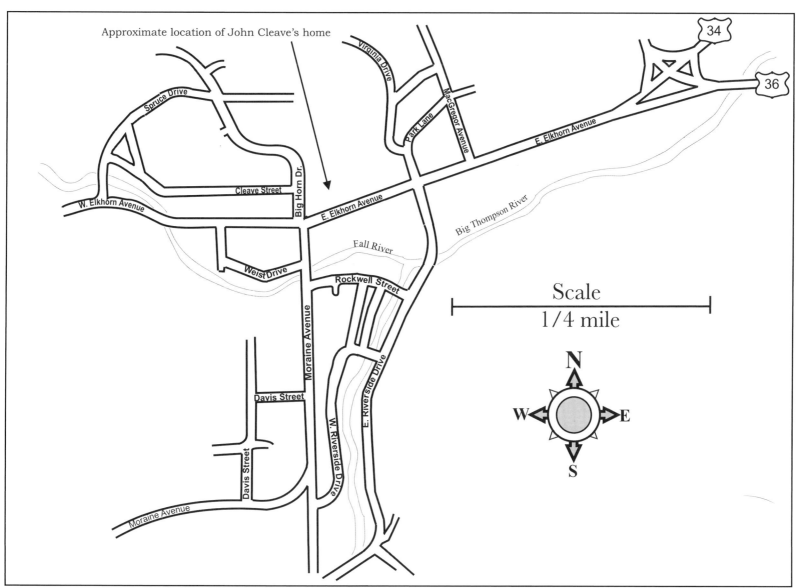

Approximate location of John Cleave's home

This is a modern-day map of Estes Park. Many of the original roads dating back to the founding of the village still exist.
(Map drawn by Kenneth Jessen)

This 1919 view of the Town of Estes Park shows that it had grown substantially since its founding in 1905 at a site selected by Cornelius H. Bond and his investment partners. (Estes Park Museum 69.24.14)

CHAPTER ONE

ESTES PARK'S
FIRST SETTLER

There isn't any record of when the first white man set foot in the park, but it might have been a trapper scouting the area for fur traders. The first recorded discovery of the park, however, was made by Joel Estes. This Kentucky-born farmer married Patsy Stollings in 1826 and raised 13 children. In 1849, Joel and his oldest son, Hardin, set out for California, with thousands of other "Forty Niners" in search of gold. Unlike the majority of prospectors, they staked out a profitable claim, which they were able to sell for $30,000 during a time when wages were $1.50 a day. This made the Estes family relatively rich. In 1855, Joel Estes left his family once again for Oregon and California, but returned empty handed. Still anxious to strike it rich, Estes, his wife, and six of their children headed to Colorado in 1859, lured by news of a gold strike in the Pikes Peak region.

The Estes family arrived in Denver on June 15, but Joel Estes was not impressed with the gold deposits there. The family settled temporarily in Golden, then turned to farming and ranching near Fort Lupton.

The only hint that Joel Estes saw of previous occupation by humans was teepees, probably of Ute origin. (Estes Park Museum, Fred Payne Clatworthy EP627)

1

Unencumbered by development, this is how Estes Park looked to Joel Estes and his family. The photograph was taken by William Henry Jackson in 1873, looking west with the Big Thompson River in the foreground. The town of Estes Park would develop in the distance. (United States Geological Survey jwh01409)

Colleen Estes Cassell writes in her book, *The Golden Pioneer – Biography of Joel Estes*, "In October 1859, Joel took at least one of his sons, Milton, and possibly all four, on a hunting and prospecting trip to the mountains." They traveled west into the foothills somewhere between the Little Thompson River and North St. Vrain Creek. Both of these drainages have deep canyons as they exit the foothills, and the Estes party probably traversed across the hills, eventually dropping down to the Little Thompson River. They followed the river into Little Elk Park (site of present-day Pinewood Springs), then up the gentle meadow in Muggins Gulch and over Park Hill where they looked down into an unoccupied valley. Joel Estes thought this was North Park, but after a few days of exploration, he concluded it was a new, unexplored valley. They found the remains of lodge poles left by Indians, but no sign of a white man's presence.

Another early view by William Henry Jackson of the Estes Park area shows the pristine valley void of civilization, with high mountains dominating the background, providing visitors a feeling of wilderness. (United State Geological Survey jwh01285)

This photograph was taken from Park Hill. Joel Estes first saw this view in 1859, the same year John Gregory struck gold ore near Central City. (Denver Public Library, Western History Department F46506)

William Newton Byers was not only the founder and editor of the Rocky Mountain News, but was a mountaineer and adventurer. When he came to Estes Park in 1864 to climb Longs Peak, he stayed with the Estes family and upon his return to Denver, named the park for them. (Colorado Historical Society F7362)

Estes determined that this remote, high valley was going to be his new home, and in 1860, he moved his family to the park. While they lived in a tent, Estes and his sons constructed two log cabins near Fish Creek, taking possession of the land as squatters since the area had not been surveyed. Estes brought about 60 head of cattle from his Fort Lupton ranch up the trail he had blazed.

The specific location Estes selected is a short distance south of today's junction of Fish Creek Road and U.S. 36 along the eastern shore of the south arm of Lake Estes.

Faced with a short growing season, Estes realized that raising cattle would be difficult and turned toward harvesting the abundant deer and elk to sell in Denver. Estes found he could make a profit on as much wild game as he could kill. By 1863, Joel had improved the trail from the park to the base of the foothills, but the round trip to Denver still required four days.

In August 1864, William N. Byers, along with three companions, used the primitive trail forged by Estes to reach the park. Editor and founder of the *Rocky Mountain News*, Byers had an adventurous spirit.

Located near the intersection of U.S. 36 and Fish Creek Road, this monument marks the site of the Estes family squatter's claim. (Kenneth Jessen)

During this trip, Byers met Joel Estes and one of his sons along the trail. Byers continued on to the cabins where he met Patsy Estes and the other children. The family had not seen a single other person that year and eagerly welcomed the Byers party. The editor, no doubt, provided the Estes family with the latest news from the outside world. When Byers returned to his Denver office, he said this of the place, "Eventually, this park will become a favorite pleasure resort." In the process, he named it Estes Park for the hospitable family he had met.

It is one thing to be a summer tourist in Estes Park and enjoy the mountains, staying in the comfort of a nice lodge, but quite another to be at the mercy of the elements. During the severe winter of 1864–1865, the Estes family decided to move back to the plains. In April 1866, the parents and children made their way over Park Hill and down Muggins Gulch using the very trail Estes blazed to get to their mountain cabins. They never returned and went on to live out their lives ranching in Huerfano County, Colorado.

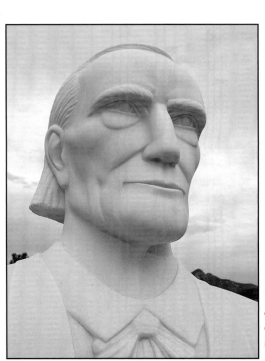

The pioneering spirit of Joel Estes is captured in the marble bust located east of the Estes Park Museum. (Kenneth Jessen)

One of two early images taken by Denver photographer William G. Chamberlain shows the home of Griff Evans constructed on Joel Estes' squatter's claim. The smaller cabins on the left might have been built by Estes. This area is now under the south end of Lake Estes. (Denver Public Library X-19337)

In Chamberlain's south-facing photograph with Longs Peak in the distance, a primitive cabin can be seen across the pond.
The pond was created by damming Fish Creek after Griff Evans took over the Estes claim in 1867. (Denver Public Library X-19303)

CHAPTER TWO

First
Tourist Business

In 1867, Griff Evans purchased the squatter's claim vacated the year before by Joel Estes. Either by design or by accident, Evans became the first in the area to promote a tourist business by offering cabins for rent. This had a lasting and profound effect on the economy of the valley and the subsequent formation of the town of Estes Park.

Evans, his wife, Jane, and five children moved into the two primitive cabins built by Estes. Evans had been swindled out of his savings by a dishonest partner, leaving him in debt. When he arrived in Estes Park, he was so poor that he did not even own the pack mules used to carry his household items. Captain George Brown helped Evans move and described the household goods as one broken stove, two chairs, a table missing a leaf, some bedding and absolutely no provisions.

No doubt, the Evans family suffered greatly during the first few years trying to make a living. Much like Joel Estes, part of their income came from supplying the Denver market with fresh game. Eventually Evans saved enough to purchase a team and a few cattle.

Located on the eastern edge of the park along Fish Creek, the Evans ranch was the first inhabited place a visitor saw after dropping down from Park Hill. While living in the Estes cabins, Evans constructed a comfortable cabin for his family with wings on either side.

Griff Evans was the pioneer of the Estes Park tourist industry and assumed title to the original Joel Estes property along Fish Creek. His reputation was tarnished when he shot and killed Rocky Mountain Jim Nugent, but Evans was acquitted of any wrongdoing. (Courtesy of Richard Evans)

7

Griff Evans and his family took over the ranch once operated by Joel Estes. The Evans cabin, with wings on either side, is show in this woodcut from Isabella Bird's A Lady's Life in the Rocky Mountains. *(Kenneth Jessen collection)*

Once Evans moved his family into the new cabins, other cabins were freed up for rental. Isabella Bird, a world traveler, adventurer and author, stayed in one of the rental cabins in 1873. She provided a vivid account of the family and noted that Griff was half hunter, half stockman. She described Evans and his wife Jane as, "... jovial, hearty Welsh people...who laugh with loud, cheery British laughs, sing in parts down to the youngest child, are free hearted and hospitable." As for Evans, she used the words, "...short and small, hospitable, careless, reckless, jolly, social, peppery, good-natured, nobody's enemy but his own." She added that Griff Evans was a sure shot and an expert hunter, a bold mountaineer, a good rider and a great cook. As for his wife, Bird noted that she was quite young and said that she worked like a slave.

This later view of the Estes-Evans-Dunraven ranch appears after it was sold to the Estes Park Company Limited in 1878. Shown are some of the first structures built in the valley, well before the town of Estes Park was established. (Rocky Mountain National Park)

Bird described the Evans cabin as having a flat roof covered with mud. Photographic evidence, however, shows that the cabin had a peaked roof-possibly as a result of subsequent improvements. The main room was good sized with a rough stone fireplace. To one side was a bedroom and on the other side, a dining area so small, the family and guests had to eat in shifts.

Bird no doubt enjoyed her stay as one of the area's earliest tourists, with fresh meat served daily along with home-baked bread. She was impressed with the clean hay for her bed along with six blankets in her rented cabin near the lake, which she called her "Queen Anne Mansion."

It was tiny and kept warm by a fire burning in a stone fireplace. Besides the bed, the room had a chair with a washbasin, and a window that looked out over the lake. The only discomfort she reported was during snowstorms. There was so little chinking that the snow accumulated inside the cabin and had to be swept out. All Evans asked was $8 a week, including meals.

In 1874, Evans shot to death a local character, Rocky Mountain Jim Nugent. Evans was acquitted in a Fort Collins court of any wrongdoing, but it tarnished his reputation in the Estes Park area. Nugent's life was immortalized by Isabella Bird in her book, *A Lady's Life in the Rocky Mountains*, where she described Nugent hauling her up Longs Peak.

This same year, Evans purchased the St. Vrain Hotel in Longmont. With the recent arrival of the Colorado Central, Longmont was connected directly to the Golden-Denver area by rail. The hotel was a good investment.

Jane Evans took over as Estes Park postmistress in March 1877. By getting the commission, she moved the post office from the MacGregor Ranch to the Estes-Evans Ranch. The post office had only been open since the previous year, and its abrupt move was quite unusual. In 1881, the MacGregors unsuccessfully tried to reclaim the post office.

The tenure of Jane Evans as postmistress lasted a little over a year, when the Evans family elected to sell their claim and leave Estes Park. The land and buildings were sold to Theodore Whyte, agent for the Earl of Dunraven's Estes Park Company Limited. Contemporary Historian James Pickering speculates in his book, *This Blue Hollow*, that lack of schooling for the Evans children probably played a role in the family's departure.

No longer were the Estes-Evans cabins rented to tourists. The site became the headquarters for the Estes Park Limited Company, owned by the Earl of Dunraven and managed by Theodore Whyte. Whyte built a home and a second structure, referred to as the Dunraven chapel, which served as the ranch headquarters. This compound would remain the largest concentration of buildings in the area until the town of Estes Park developed.

This view shows the ornate "Dunraven chapel" (right-center) that served as ranch headquarters for the Estes Park Company Limited.
The shed in the center has a bay window and smaller cabins in the background may have provided housing for ranch hands.
(Denver Public Library X-8292)

In 1890, the Estes-Evans-Dunraven ranch included Theodore Whyte's home.
The ranch headquarters are on the right behind the shed. (Estes Park Museum EP632)

CHAPTER THREE

ESTES PARK
BEGINNINGS

In 1875, John Cleave from Cornwall, England, settled in the park along Fish Creek, where he took up a 160-acre homestead. He worked for Theodore Whyte as a carpenter, first constructing Dunraven's cottage in 1876 followed by the Estes Park Hotel. Both of these structures were south of the Joel Estes homestead site. In 1885, Cleave traded his homestead to the Estes Park Company Limited for an equivalent number of acres at the confluence of the Big Thompson and Fall Rivers. Cleave's original homestead was in an open meadow suitable for ranching, while the confluence of the two rivers was rocky and bounded by cliffs.

Although school had been taught at the Elkhorn Lodge since 1881, it wasn't until 1883 that a school district was formed. School was held in a converted guest cabin starting with 15 school-age children. The cabin was used until 1886 when a proper schoolhouse was constructed at the intersection of primary roads through the area on John Cleave's newly acquired land. The schoolhouse was 22-foot by 40-foot, made of milled lumber with tall windows on either side, typical of schools at the time. The building also served as a community building and doubled as a church on Sundays.

The same year Cleave acquired his new holdings he became the Estes Park postmaster. He constructed a double-gabled building across from the school and the post office was soon moved to this location. The east side of this building was rented out and the post office occupied the west end of the structure.

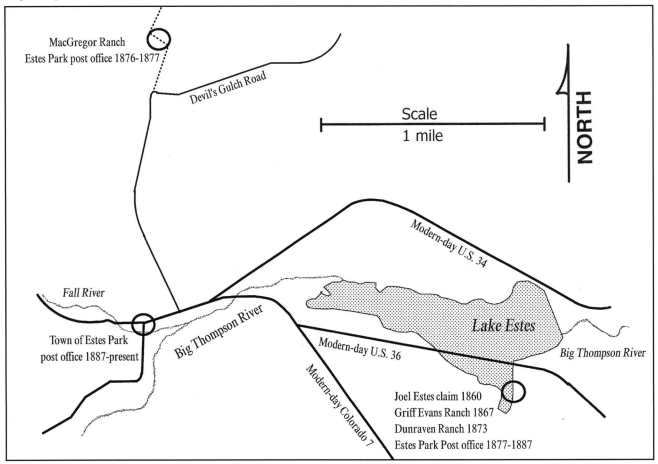

MacGregor Ranch
Estes Park post office 1876-1877

Devil's Gulch Road

Scale
1 mile

NORTH

Modern-day U.S. 34

Fall River

Town of Estes Park
post office 1887-present

Big Thompson River

Modern-day U.S. 36

Lake Estes

Big Thompson River

Modern-day Colorado 7

Joel Estes claim 1860
Griff Evans Ranch 1867
Dunraven Ranch 1873
Estes Park Post office 1877-1887

*Opened in 1876, the first location for the Estes Park post office was at the MacGregor Ranch on the north end of the valley.
In 1877, it was moved southeast to the Estes-Evans-Dunraven ranch, a site now under the waters of Lake Estes. In 1887,
the post office was moved once again to what grew into Estes Park. (Map drawn by Kenneth Jessen)*

In 1888, Cleave constructed his home next to the school. It was similar in architecture to the combination store/post office, only smaller. A photograph taken in 1903 indicates that Cleave added several lean-tos at the rear of his home.

Looking at the valley, the logical place for a new community might have been at the Estes-Evans-Dunraven ranch where vast meadows extended in all directions. This land, however, was owned by the Earl of Dunraven. The property Cleave got was

This is the future site of Estes Park looking west in 1903. It was referred to as "The Corners." Postmaster John Cleave lived in the frame house on the right-hand side of the road. West of his home is the school/community building. Across from Cleave's home (to the left) is the combination store/post office, also constructed by Cleave. In the distance, just visible through the trees, is a livery stable. The ownership of other structures is unknown. (Colorado Historical Society)

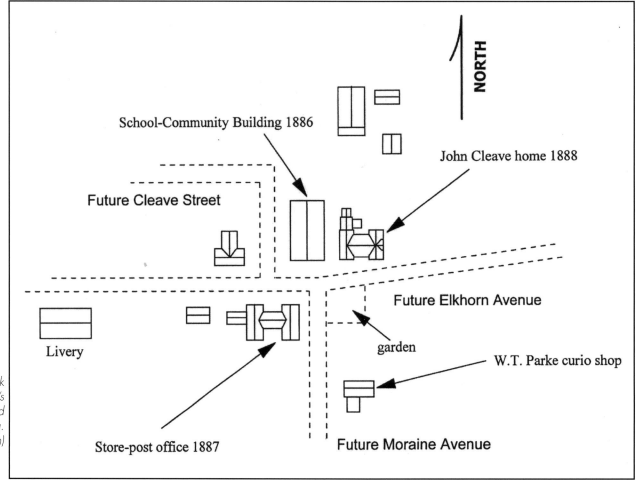

School-Community Building 1886

John Cleave home 1888

Future Cleave Street

NORTH

Future Elkhorn Avenue

garden

W.T. Parke curio shop

Livery

Store-post office 1887

Future Moraine Avenue

This is how the future Estes Park looked in 1903 with John Cleave's home, the store/post office and the school/community building. (Map drawn by Kenneth Jessen)

picturesque and as a bonus, was located at the intersection of three major roads through the area. One road headed southeast over Park Hill. A second road headed south along the Big Thompson River a short distance, then turned west toward Beaver Point and ended in Moraine Park. The third road headed west past the Elkhorn Lodge following the Fall River to Horseshoe Park. There was probably a trail coming in from the north as well. Cleave's land included the confluence of the area's two major streams as well, adding to its appeal.

Copied from a 1902 album, this image shows a horse-drawn covered passenger wagon arriving in front of the Estes Park post office. The post office shared its space with a store. (Estes Park Museum sb63)

The cluster of buildings at this intersection was known as "The Corners," a busy place during the summer with the arrival of horse-drawn passenger wagons and stage-coaches with tourists bound for outlying lodges. Whether it was his intention or not, Cleave's land became the nucleus for the town of Estes Park and is identified by the very same intersection, today's Elkhorn and Moraine Avenues.

A 1903 photograph shows the handful of structures located at "The Corners" included the combination post office/general store, school/community building and John Cleave's home. In 1900, William T. Parke opened a small store on the east side of the future Moraine Avenue south of the intersection. It was the first store to remain open all year. He sold it to Samuel Service the following year.

Later, Parke became Estes Park's first resident photographer housed in a false-front building on the north side of Elkhorn Avenue.

Other buildings also show up in this photograph including a livery stable and several structures of unknown ownership. John Cleave owned all of the land, and it can be assumed that he leased parcels to others. It wasn't until 1905 when Cleave sold his property that the town of Estes Park was surveyed.

The 1886 school-community building was later moved a short distance west and converted into the studio of Fredrick Payne Clatworthy. Amazing after all the growth in Estes Park, this structure remains standing although hardly recognizable.

Taken in 1902-1903, this shows "The Corners" looking south with John Cleave's home in the left foreground. To the right is the 1886 school/community building with the double-gabled store/ post office across the road. (The Crags collection)

Sam Service arrived in the village in 1901 and as mentioned, purchased William T. Parke's general store. Service quickly realized that Parke's store was too small and constructed what became the largest building in Estes Park for many years. His new store, located on the north side of Elkhorn Avenue and Virginia Drive, was completed in 1906. It remains standing.

In 1905, Cleave was ready to move on, having served faithfully as Estes Park postmaster for 20 years. He sold his property to a group of businessmen including Cornelius Bond, who had formed the Estes Park Town Company and had begun the incorporation of Estes Park. Abner Sprague was the surveyor and today, the town retains many of the same traits he mapped in the early 1900s.

This view shows John Cleave's home with the arrival of several horse-drawn stages. The photograph has been touched up to emphasize "The Highlands" on the closest wagon. (Estes Park Museum EP476)

The characteristic bend in Elkhorn Avenue at its intersection with Moraine Avenue continues to be an identifiable feature, for example. Several other streets leading to Elkhorn Avenue were also identified and named at this time.

 The problem faced by Sprague was that the area was constrained by a narrow, rugged canyon with a cliff on the south side, a steep slope on the north side and the imposing bulk of Prospect Mountain in the middle. This left little in the way of level ground suitable for building. As impractical as the location seems, the confined space and rugged surroundings give Estes Park its unique characteristics.

The town company put up 264 lots for sale, and sales were brisk as entrepreneurs gambled on the success of the town. Several enterprisers set up tents while their frame stores were under construction, and these tents are evident in early images.

At first glance, John Cleave's home seems architecturally simple. It is a pair of gabled buildings sitting side-by-side with a connecting structure. There was only one dormer on the east side and not centered in the roof. The connecting structure was set back from the front and its roof peak did not line up with the roof peak on the dormer. The front entrance was on the south side from a small porch. (Drawing by Kenneth Jessen)

It is assumed that the merchants who predated the 1905 formation of the town company purchased their lots.

Many of the logs used for building came from a burn in Mill Creek Basin and milled lumber was hauled in from area sawmills. Premier photographer Fred Payne Clatworthy was not the least bit impressed with early Estes Park construction. He commented that the only requirement for these structures is that they shed water and support the weight of a sign!

By 1917, when Estes Park was incorporated, it had grown quickly into a quaint village fueled by a tourist-based economy with homes, lodges, stores and restaurants.

From his book, *America's Switzerland*, author James H. Pickering says, "In a little more than a decade, the town had established a visible footprint that would be recognizable to visitors returning fifty or seventy-five years later." Pickering continues, "Aesthetics scarcely mattered. Estes Park's quickly earned reputation as a quaint and attractive resort community was clearly due to its picturesque mountain setting, not the architectural tastes, talents, or vision of its early builders."

Today, with virtually every square inch of Sprague's initial survey occupied by shops, time seems to have stood still, giving contemporary visitors the feel of a small mountain village with a European flavor.

*This 1888 image shows the National Education Association at the Estes Park schoolhouse.
The photograph was taken two years after the building was constructed. (Denver Public Library X-8279)*

This 1896 view of Estes Park is looking east and shows the schoolhouse in the center with the twin roof peaks of the combination store/post office just visible to the right and immediately left of the barn. (Denver Public Library X-8270)

This 1904 image is looking east, taken a year before Estes Park was platted by the Estes Park Town Company. The community building is hidden in the left-center by a tree and beyond it is John Cleave's home. The store/post office is right-center and to the extreme right-center is W. T. Parke's curio shop, at this time owned by Sam Service. (Denver Public Library, Western History Department F16613)

This is the second in a series of photographs taken by Fred Payne Clatworthy looking west; this one in 1907. There are a few Stanley Steamers on the right and on the left, the drug store of Dr. Weist with its horizontal siding. At the end of the row of buildings on the left is the Kandy Kitchen.
(Estes Park Museum, Fred Payne Clatworthy)

This Fred Payne Clatworthy photograph was taken in 1906 looking west on Elkhorn Avenue. There aren't any automobiles, only horse-drawn wagons, including the Loveland Estes Park Stage Company. John Cleave's home is on the right and the combination store/post office on the left. (Estes Park Museum, Fred Payne Clatworthy)

In this 1908 image, Stanley Steamers dominate the Clatworthy photograph of Elkhorn Avenue. They are all loaded with tourists who probably just arrived from one of several railroad depots. On the far right is the corner of the brand new Estes Park Bank. (Estes Park Museum, Fred Payne Clatworthy EP411)

This 1908 image was taken looking west with the new schoolhouse on the right, constructed in 1907.
The long white building in the mid-distance with a road leading directly to it was the store built by Sam Service.
(Denver Public Library, Western History Department, Louis McClure F34045)

When Denver photographer Louis McClure took this 1908 image looking east down Elkhorn Avenue, the village was starting to take shape. The tent closest to the photographer was the temporary home of the Loveland-Estes Park Transportation Company. Other tents may have been occupied by merchants as their summer quarters. (Denver Public Library, Western History Department Mc1005)

With its characteristic bend in Elkhorn Avenue, this image shows the Manford Hotel on the left and the Hupp Hotel on the right. John Cleave's home is clearly visible on the far left center. To the right of Cleave's home is the new fire bell tower. Partially obscured and above the left-center tree is Sam Service's store. Mount Olympus is on the right skyline. (Estes Park Museum EP013)

In this 1908 view of Estes Park, the false front of Boyd's livery stable facing Riverside Drive is partially blocked by the barn in the foreground. The Boyd home is just above the stable and slightly to the right. Sam Service's general store, with its ornate false front, is right-center with advertising on both its roof and east-facing side. The Service home is immediately to the left (west). (Estes Park Museum 76.3.3)

By 1909, the Presbyterian Church had been constructed on west Elkhorn Avenue. In the summer of 1911 the large tree along Elkhorn Avenue
that appears in the previous images was removed. The Loveland-Estes Park Auto Company garage is in the left corner,
a building that would be replaced in 1915 by a cement block structure. (Estes Park Museum 70.28.4)

Looking west shows Elkhorn Avenue running diagonally toward Sam Service's store. The Estes Park Steam Laundry is the small false front building at the far left. The Boyd and Macdonald homes are facing the Sam Service store in the center of the photograph. (Estes Park Museum 86.7.3)

Dated at 1910, Freelan Stanley's Estes Park Transportation Company can be seen in the middle-left with Sam Service's store on the extreme right facing Elkhorn Avenue. Boyd's blacksmith shop is in the lower right, and the Boyd home is immediately above. The building with lettering on its roof left-center is the Macdonald lumberyard. The Manford Hotel is the large building with the veranda in the center of this view looking west-northwest. (Estes Park Museum)

In this 1910 view looking north, Malmburg's Livery facing Elkhorn Avenue is on the right and Boyd's home is on the far left with Boyd's blacksmith shop lower-left. The new schoolhouse can be seen in the middle-right. The single-track dirt road running across the middle of this view is Park Avenue. (Estes Park Museum)

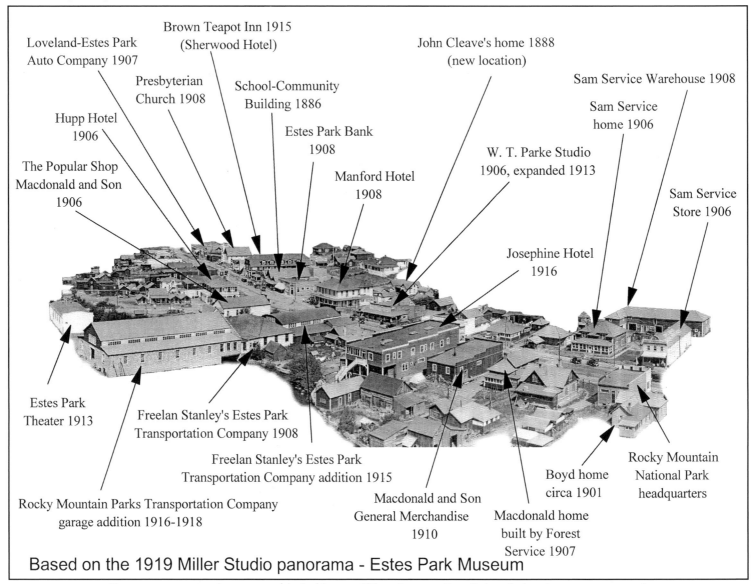

Loveland-Estes Park
Auto Company 1907

Brown Teapot Inn 1915
(Sherwood Hotel)

John Cleave's home 1888
(new location)

Presbyterian
Church 1908

School-Community
Building 1886

Sam Service Warehouse 1908

Sam Service
home 1906

Hupp Hotel
1906

Estes Park Bank
1908

W. T. Parke Studio
1906, expanded 1913

The Popular Shop
Macdonald and Son
1906

Manford Hotel
1908

Sam Service
Store 1906

Josephine Hotel
1916

Estes Park
Theater 1913

Freelan Stanley's Estes Park
Transportation Company 1908

Freelan Stanley's Estes Park
Transportation Company addition 1915

Rocky Mountain Parks Transportation Company
garage addition 1916-1918

Macdonald and Son
General Merchandise
1910

Macdonald home
built by Forest
Service 1907

Boyd home
circa 1901

Rocky Mountain
National Park
headquarters

Based on the 1919 Miller Studio panorama - Estes Park Museum

*This composite image shows many of the buildings on Elkhorn Avenue in Estes Park and when they were constructed.
(Composite by Kenneth Jessen)*

CHAPTER FOUR

HOTELS AND LODGES

Without places for visitors to stay, Estes Park could not have evolved into a tourist center. This is an overview of early lodges and hotels in and near the town.

Elkhorn Lodge, late 1870s

The Elkhorn Lodge, located immediately west of Estes Park, played an important role in the success of the village. The Elkhorn provided a rustic experience for visitors, yet after the village grew, guests were within walking distance of the hub of town. The Elkhorn Lodge, however, has a convoluted history starting with pioneer William Edwin James who worked in the forestry business in New York State. James changed careers to selling groceries after his marriage to Ella McCabe, but the 1873 recession forced him to seek yet another fresh start. While on a hunting trip to Estes Park, he became enthralled with the area and decided that this mountain valley would be his next home. Like others who came to the park, he planned on raising cattle. James brought his wife west in 1874 and they built a modest homestead cabin at a place later called McCreery Spring. Its location is a short distance north of the present-day Devil's Gulch Road, and the cabin remains standing.

William James constructed this homestead cabin in 1874 north of Devil's Gulch Road and later traded it for land along the Fall River owned by Rev. William McCreery. In this 1892 photograph, the McCreery family is shown relaxing at the cabin, which remains standing. (Estes Park Museum)

Cabins were built to supplement the James family income when they began accepting guests at their cattle ranch in 1878. This was many years in advance of the founding of Estes Park. (Rocky Mountain National Park)

James then got a lucky break: Loveland minister Rev. William H. McCreery had land along the Fall River immediately west of the future town of Estes Park. Although the open meadow was suitable for ranching, McCreery only wanted a weekend retreat and the James cabin was perfect for that. In 1876, James and McCreery shook hands and swapped land.

James and his wife eagerly constructed a home on their new, lush meadowland. Although his original objective for the land was raising cattle, tourists began stopping at the James ranch wanting a place to camp or some food to quiet their growling stomachs. So in 1878 Ella James began hosting guests to supplement their income. Tents were set up as the first accommodations followed by the construction of a lodge and cabins for rent. The resort grew every year by one or two cabins and by and by, the income from the guests exceeded that from ranching.

Since elk roamed freely through the ranch to winter pasture and back across the property into the high country every spring, it was logical for the Jameses to call their central building the Elkhorn Lodge. By 1880, the resort could host up to 40 guests. Cold, running water was brought to the cabins and later, hot water was supplied. Each cabin had its own private outhouse.

The land around McCreery Spring was not suitable for cattle, so James selected another location – a broader meadow with plenty of water – to the west, in the Black Canyon. He claimed 80 acres and erected his second cabin. Unfortunately for the James family, Denver lawyer Alexander Q. MacGregor discovered the Black Canyon in 1872 and homesteaded much of the area. MacGregor's mother-in-law, Georgianna Heeney, had her own homestead claim adjacent to the MacGregor claim, and it overlapped a portion of the James claim, blocking its access.

The original Elkhorn Lodge was constructed in the late 1870s and it, along with rental cabins, became the primary source of income for the James family. This building remains standing, but no longer functions as a lodge. (Rocky Mountain National Park)

A contemporary photograph of the old Elkhorn Lodge shows few changes over the years. A new larger building, constructed around 1900, succeeded this structure as the lodge. (Kenneth Jessen)

As their family of four children grew, the Jameses made sure they received a proper education. At first, a family member taught the students. In the meantime, Rev. McCreery became Larimer County Superintendent of Schools. In 1883, the Jameses applied to establish an Estes Park school district, which was quickly approved by McCreery, and without haste, one of the Elkhorn Lodge cottages was converted into a schoolhouse. In 1886, and significant to the future of Estes Park, a new school was built on John Cleave's land near the confluence of the Big Thompson and Fall Rivers. James and his three sons helped with its construction.

After the death of William James in 1894, his wife Ella and their children continued hosting tourists. Additions to the Elkhorn Lodge compound in 1907 and again in 1912 brought the Elkhorn's capacity to 180 guests. Today, many of its original buildings remain standing including the first lodge constructed in the late 1870s.

Estes Park's first school was originally a guest cabin at the Elkhorn Lodge and was converted into classrooms in 1883. It functioned as a school until 1886 when a new schoolhouse was constructed at the future site of Estes Park. (Kenneth Jessen)

Hupp Hotel, 1906

Although the Elkhorn Lodge had been in operation since the late 1870s, it wasn't until after Estes Park was platted in 1905 that development of the town began. In 1906, the 23-room Hupp Hotel was constructed on the southwest corner of Elkhorn and Moraine Avenues spanning four lots where once stood the combination store/post office built by John Cleave in 1887 (coincident with the relocation of the post office from the Estes-Evans-Dunraven ranch on Fish Creek). To please the guests of the Hupp Hotel, Josephine Hupp, her niece and her niece's husband opened an ice cream and baked goods store nearby.

Contemporary historian James H. Pickering explains problems with the name of the Hupp Hotel. "The confusion began in 1908 when Josie Hupp purchased the new Manford Hotel diagonally across the street from her Hupp Hotel.

In 1906, the 23-room Hupp Hotel was constructed on the southwest corner of Elkhorn and Moraine Avenues spanning four lots where the store/post office once stood. (Bobbie Heisterkamp postcard collection)

39

The Manford Hotel, built in 1908, was sold and renamed the Hupp Annex after only one season. It was located on the northeast corner of Elkhorn Avenue and Big Horn Drive. The building still stands. Just visible to the left is John Cleave's home. (Bobbie Heisterkamp postcard collection)

Manford Hotel, 1908

In 1907, John Manford purchased the lot where John Cleave's home was located, then moved the building north to the rear of the property to make room for a 21-room hotel. The Manford Hotel, located on the northeast corner of Big Horn Drive and Elkhorn Avenue, was completed the following year. Manford constructed his hotel to be larger than rival Hupp Hotel across the intersection, taking up six lots with a veranda that wrapped around its corner. After just one season, Manford sold the hotel to his competitor, Josephine Hupp. She quickly changed the name to the Hupp Annex. Incidentally, Cleave's home was razed in 1947.

The Manford Hotel remains standing, but its veranda has long been replaced by storefronts.

She promptly changed the Manford's name to the Hupp Annex, as it was known until 1932 through two changes of ownership, despite the fact that the old Hupp Hotel was now the Estes Park Hotel. Now there was a Hupp Annex, but no Hupp Hotel." The 15-room, second story of the original Hupp Hotel was leased by the subsequent owner of the Hupp Annex. She then switched the names so that the Hupp Annex became the Hupp Hotel and visa versa.

Stanley Hotel, 1909

The Stanley Hotel is the icon of Estes Park, overlooking the town with its commanding, unobstructed view of the mountains. It was the first electrified hotel in the world and its inaugural opening was in 1909 for a pharmaceutical convention. Built for an estimated half-million dollars, the 92-room hotel was also

The Stanley Hotel, the most elaborate and expensive hotel in the area, dominated the area northeast of the Town of Estes Park.
It became a symbol for the town. (Rocky Mountain National Park)

one of the most expensive hotels constructed in the United States. Other buildings
on the site included the casino, carriage house, manager's house, staff dormitories and
utility buildings. The following year, a scaled-down duplicate of the hotel, called the
Manor House, was finished a short distance east of the hotel.

Due to minimal heating, the Stanley Hotel was open only from June to September.
The rest of the year, guests stayed in the fully heated Manor House. At $5 to $8 a day
depending on the room, the Stanley Hotel was by far the most expensive place to stay
in the Estes Park area with other hotels charging $1 to $2 a day.

The Lewiston Hotel was constructed on an outcropping north of Elkhorn Avenue at the extreme west end of town. A.D. Lewis started small with a few rental cabins, which led to the expansion of their home into a hotel. It was destroyed by fire in 1941. (Estes Park Museum 84.32.35)

Its builder and architect, Freelan Stanley, came to Estes Park to recover from tuberculosis. He quickly regained his health and started planning to make Estes Park a major tourist destination. After completing a series of architectural drawings for his hotel, Stanley settled on the Georgian Colonial Revival style. This was in sharp contrast to the surrounding primitive-looking lodges that could be classified as "Rocky Mountain rustic."

Construction began in 1907 using lumber from both the Griffith sawmill near Bierstadt Lake and one in Hidden Valley. As the hotel started to take shape, Stanley named it "The Dunraven." At one time, the Earl of Dunraven controlled thousands of acres in the Estes Park area, but some of the land was obtained illegally. Due to the Earl's tarnished reputation, residents objected and convinced Stanley to name the hotel after himself.

Lewiston Hotel, 1913

This hotel once sat on a rocky ridge above the west end of the Estes Park business district. It started out as the home of Augustus D. Lewis who came to Estes Park in 1912 and worked as a cashier at the Estes Park Bank. In 1913, Lewis and his wife decided to enter the resort business by building rental bungalows around their home. This led to the expansion of their home in stages starting in 1915, and by 1920, the hotel included 70 rooms. Lewis formed the Lewiston Hotel Company, which included the chalets near Marys Lake, businesses in downtown Estes Park including the Lewiston Café, and the Josephine Hotel. In 1941, a fire destroyed the Lewiston Hotel beyond repair. Townhouses occupy the site today.

Crags Lodge, 1914

The story of the Crags Lodge is tied to the life of Joe Mills, born in Fort Scott, Kansas in 1880. Much like his older brother Enos Mills, Joe wanted to live his life as a naturalist. At the age of 16, his parents gave him permission to spend a summer in Colorado near the base of Longs Peak with his uncle, Reverend Elkanah Lamb. When Joe reached the mountains, he thought that the stagecoach to Estes Park was reasonably priced, but elected to purchase a bicycle as his mode of transportation. Over the Bald Mountain-Pole Hill Road west of Loveland, he pedaled to his uncle's ranch. Young Mills worked at his uncle's Longs Peak House and explored the surrounding mountains during his spare time. He built a small cabin near Cabin Rock, while brother Enos purchased the Longs Peak House and turned it into a first class resort.

To accommodate Longs Peak hikers, Joe started construction on the Timberline House located near Jim's Grove on the Longs Peak trail. Enos finished construction in 1908. It was an overnight stop for clients who had hired a guide.

After a career in athletics, Mills wanted to return to Colorado, so in 1909 he leased the Forks Hotel in Drake. He and his wife, Ethel, operated the hotel until 1913 at which time they purchased land on the north side of Prospect Mountain above Estes Park. They constructed the Crags Hotel, which opened on July 4, 1914 after one of the most severe winters on record. In 1921, Joe Mills purchased additional land and added to the facilities at the Crags, including a recreation hall.

As a teenager, Joe Mills constructed this small cabin on the flank of Twin Sisters, not far from his brother's cabin. Both Joe and Enos Mills worked at their uncle's lodge, the Longs Peak House, before Enos purchased it. (Crags Lodge collection)

After managing the Forks Hotel in Drake for a number of years, Joe Mills and his wife, Ethel, constructed the Crags Lodge above Estes Park. It opened on July 4, 1914 and remains a popular place today. (Fred Payne Clatworthy, Crags Lodge collection)

When Mills accepted a position at the University of Colorado, the family moved to a house on Baseline Road in Boulder, but continued to operate the Crags Lodge.

Joe Mills passed away in 1935 at the age of 55. His death was the result of fatal injuries incurred in a head-on collision with a Denver tramway car on Colfax Avenue. The hotel remained in the Mills family until 1941 when it closed during World War II. It was leased in 1945 and then sold in 1947. After several changes in ownership, the Crags Lodge became part of the Arizona-based Golden Eagle Resorts.

Prospect Inn, 1915

Located at the corner of Park Avenue and Virginia Drive, the Prospect Inn started as the Dutch Kitchen. Its owner, Stella Miller, constructed the inn to the west of her kitchen. The two-story inn could accommodate about 25 guests and included a spacious dinning hall, 45 feet by 30 feet.

Sherwood Hotel, 1915

The Sherwood Hotel started on the north side of Elkhorn Avenue as the Brown Teapot Inn in 1915. In 1921, it became the Sherwood Hotel and two years later, Josephine Hupp purchased the place. It was managed by "Johnny" Baker who, at one time, had toured with Buffalo Bill Cody. The hotel burned to the ground in 1956 and was not rebuilt.

Josephine Hotel, 1916

Josephine Hupp built the three-story Josephine Hotel in 1916 along the south side of Elkhorn Avenue and east of the intersection with Moraine Avenue. After a decade, Hupp sold the hotel to the Lewiston Hotel Company. In 1926, Hupp purchased the hotel back, only to sell it again in 1930. The purchaser, Ted Jelsema, renamed the Josephine Hotel the Riverside Hotel. Jelsema also owned the Riverside Amusement Park immediately behind the building. In 1956, a fire destroyed the second floor of the Josephine and that portion of the building was not reconstructed. The structure still stands west of Macdonald Book Shop.

National Park Hotel, 1919

Harriet Rogers Byerly opened the Pine Cone Tea Room in 1916 on the north side of Elkhorn Avenue. She moved the tea room to the rear of her property and constructed the 10-room National Park Hotel in 1918–1919. She expanded the structure in 1926 by constructing a second story, adding another 30 rooms for guests. After its life as a hotel, it became a *Ripley's Believe it or Not!* museum. It is now the Park Mall and has been divided into several small shops.

The Josephine Hotel, constructed in 1916, remains standing today on the south side of Elkhorn Avenue. It is now the Wheel Bar. (Estes Park Museum)

The National Park Hotel came along in 1919 and was located on the north side of Elkhorn Avenue west of the Sam Service store.
It was expanded in 1926 with the addition of a second story and the building, although somewhat altered, remains in use today as the Park Mall.
(Bobbie Heisterkamp postcard collection, W. T. Parke photographer)

CHAPTER FIVE

BUSINESSES

Without it core businesses, most of which cater to tourists, Estes Park would not have survived. Up until the past decade or so, many businesses were seasonal, shuttering their doors for all but a few months of each year. The influx of year-round residents has changed Estes Park, converting it into a tourist town for all seasons.

William T. Parke, 1900

William T. Parke opened a small store along the future Moraine Avenue to the south of the intersection with Elkhorn Avenue, which was the first store to remain open all year. Parke sold the business to Samuel Service, and in 1906, Parke moved his store to the north side of Elkhorn Avenue west of Big Horn Drive, where it remained for many years. He expanded his original false-front store in 1913 with an addition on its east side. He advertised the sale of Estes Park images, novelties, postcards, newspapers, magazines, stationary, candies, fishing tackle, postcard albums, photo albums, film, cameras and baseball equipment. He left a legacy of excellent images of Estes Park. Parke even had a circulating library.

This is W. T. Parke's store on the north side of Elkhorn Avenue west of the intersection with Big Horn Drive. It is shown after its 1913 addition. (Estes Park Museum 74.16.5)

Foot Mercantile, 1905

Elizabeth Foot was a pioneer business-woman who started her business in John Cleave's combination post office/store and then moved to a long, frame building on the southeast corner of Elkhorn and Moraine Avenues. In her second location, she advertised her store as "E. M. A. Foot's Utility and Curio Shop" selling dry goods, home furnishings, ready-to-wear clothing, boots, shoes, fishing tackle, Indian arts and crafts and, of course, postcards.

When she became seriously ill in the fall of 1908, the store's operation was turned over to Mrs. Homer James. The Macdonald family purchased the structure in 1910 and opened up their own store. A year later, the Macdonalds constructed a second store west of their home, also on the south side of Elkhorn Avenue. The bookstore, as we know it today, started in the parlor of their home.

Ye Lyttel Shop, 1905

Fred Payne Clatworthy came to Estes Park along with several family members to set up a photographic shop in the village. In 1905, Clatworthy opened up "Ye Lyttel Shop" on Elkhorn Avenue and in 1907, moved his shop to the former school/community building.

Not only did Clatworthy provide images for tourists to purchase, he also operated the village's first laundry service, sending what needed to be cleaned to Denver. He sold sporting equipment, leather goods and had a soda fountain in Ye Lyttel Shop. He became known not only for his artistic photography, but also for hand tinting his photographs. After a quarter century, he closed his doors to go into the wholesale business.

Fred Payne Clatworthy's studio and shop on Elkhorn Avenue sold a wide variety of items including Eastman film, Kodak cameras and prints. In this photograph, the shop occupies the 1886 school/community building. It had been moved several doors west from its original location.
(Estes Park Museum, Fred Payne Clatworthy)

Sam Service General Merchandise, 1906

Irish-born Sam Service changed the look of Estes Park. After he sold his grocery store in Lyons, apparently seeing better opportunities in Estes Park, he purchased William Parke's general store on the south side of Elkhorn Avenue. However, Service found that this building was too small. With grand ideas, he erected the largest building in Estes Park on the northwest corner of Elkhorn Avenue and Virginia Drive. Work was begun in 1905 and completed the following year. This general store remained the most prominent business for over two decades and could be identified by the large, white lettering across its roof, "Sam'l Service General Merchandise," along with a bold sign across the side of the building advertising hay, grain and camper's supplies. It served as a gathering place for locals with its spacious interior heated by a pot-bellied stove. Service constructed his home immediately to the west of the store, which was also completed in 1906. It is easy to identify by its porch facing Elkhorn Avenue. Later, a warehouse was built onto the rear of the store. Service added a filling station to his business in 1919, which remained in operation until 1928.

Sam Service's store became the largest structure in Estes Park and remained so for many years. It was located on the northwest corner of Elkhorn Avenue and Virginia Drive, and was opened for business in 1906. (Estes Park Museum)

Estes Park Bank, 1908

Freelan Stanley either invented or built whatever was required to achieve his goals. This included Estes Park's first power plant along the Fall River and also the town's first brick business building, the Estes Park Bank. Located on the northwest corner of Elkhorn Avenue and Big Horn Drive, the bank was incorporated in early 1908 with construction starting that spring. It was open for business in June of that year. Previously, the lot was occupied by the 1886 school/community building, which was moved to the west and became Fred Payne Clatworthy's studio. In 1910, an addition was constructed on the bank's west side, and it housed Boyd's grocery store for many years. The bank building remains standing and although modified, retains its corner entrance.

The Estes Park Bank, founded by Freelan Stanley in 1908, remains standing today and houses a camera store. It was the town's first brick building. (Bobbie Heisterkamp postcard collection)

Pine Cone Inn, 1909

On the south side of Elkhorn Avenue west of the Josephine Hotel was artist William H. Tallant's log home and studio. It became the Pine Cone Inn, a local gathering spot and eatery. It later served as the Plantation Restaurant and after a fire in 1943, was remodeled. It remains standing.

Presbyterian Church, 1909

Using a loan from the Presbyterian Board of Missions, the Presbyterian congregation purchased a lot on the north side of Elkhorn Avenue at the west end of the business district. Volunteers constructed a church there in 1909. Prior to this, services had been held in the school/community building. The church was enlarged in 1935 and remains standing as The Old Church Shops.

Popular Shop and Macdonald General Merchandise, 1910

James Edward Macdonald first visited Estes Park in 1902. After his marriage, he and his wife settled in New Jersey, but Macdonald was beleaguered with memories of his Colorado visit. The call of the mountains was too great, and in 1908, he returned to Estes Park. Macdonald purchased a log cabin on the south side of Elkhorn Avenue, built by the Forest Service the previous year. This became his family home. In 1910, he opened a hardware and general store on the southeast corner of Elkhorn and Moraine Avenues in a long frame building constructed in 1906. He called it "The Popular Shop" advertising "Fancy Groceries."

In 1928, Macdonald retired from the general store business at the age of 67 and opened a bookstore in the parlor of the family home. At that time, his son opened the Macdonald Steam Laundry. After James Edward Macdonald passed away, his wife, Jessica, continued to run the bookstore with the help of their daughters.

As the years passed, the bookstore was expanded into the entire lower floor of the family residence while the family moved to the second floor. Jessica passed away in her sleep in 1957 at the age of 83, and the bookstore was handed down

This is "The Popular Shop" advertising "Fancy Groceries," opened in 1910 by James Edward Macdonald. The store stood at the southeast corner of Elkhorn and Moraine Avenues and was constructed in 1906. Behind the building on the left is the roof of the lumberyard, also operated by the Macdonald family. (Courtesy of Paula Steige)

Macdonald and Son General Merchandise store stood immediately to the west of the Macdonald home. Today, both structures are still standing and the home on the left is now the Macdonald Book Shop. (Courtesy of Paula Steige)

The Estes Park Steam Laundry was constructed in 1908 and was originally owned and operated by Julian Johnson. In 1914, it was purchased by Ralph Macdonald. The structure was located on the south side of Elkhorn Avenue at the east end of the business district. (Courtesy of Paul Steige)

There were several businesses on the north side of Elkhorn Avenue toward the west end of town, west of the Estes Park Bank and east of the Presbyterian Church. The building on the left is the 1886 school/community building which, at the time of this photograph, was the lodge for the Independent Order of Odd Fellows. (Fred Payne Clatworthy, courtesy of Barbra Clatworthy Gish)

to her daughters, who had been helping during the busy summer months. One of the daughters, Louise Macdonald Brown, took over the operation. After her passing in 1971, the store was left to her daughter, Paula. Paula Steige and her children continue to operate the store and carry on its original tradition.

Park Theater, 1913

The Park Theater, the idea of J.L. Jackson, was partially constructed in 1913, however it was Cornelius Bond who completed the project the following year. Bond sold the theater to Fred Jackson, who operated it until 1922. The iconic tower was added a few years later by Ralph Gwynn. In October 2009, the theater was singed by the Park Theater Mall fire, but was saved from complete destruction. As one of the oldest motion picture theaters in the United States, the landmark building is on the National Register of Historic Places.

This is the school/community building when it served as a schoolhouse between 1886 and 1907.
(Estes Park Museum)

L. E. Grace Gift Shop, 1915

Lawrence E. Grace arrived in Estes Park in 1912 and opened a small shop that sold handmade items. Grace was a master carpenter and in 1915, he built a gift shop on the south side of Elkhorn Avenue west of Moraine Avenue about halfway to the end of the block. At his new shop, Grace sold items by local artists as well as his own photographs. This structure remains standing.

Businesses

By the time this photograph was taken, Lindsey F. Boettcher had switched from a plumbing shop to running an electrical supply business. This structure was located immediately west of the 1886 school/community building, the corner of which can be seen on the far right. Since the house to the left matches the store, it could be assumed that Boettcher lived in the home. (Fred Payne Clatworthy, courtesy of Barbra Clatworthy Gish)

This view of the north side of Elkhorn Avenue shows the 1907 Loveland-Estes Park Auto Company garage at the far end of the street. Next to it is the Presbyterian Church constructed in 1908. A restaurant and a meat market occupy the lots closet to the photographer. (Fred Payne Clatworthy, courtesy of Barbra Clatworthy Gish)

CHAPTER SIX

ROCKY MOUNTAIN NATIONAL PARK
ESTABLISHED

Certainly the biggest impact on the Estes Park area was the opening of Rocky Mountain National Park in 1915. This single event solidified Estes Park's position as a tourist gateway.

Rocky Mountain National Park

The creation of Rocky Mountain National Park was spearheaded by a passionate individual, Enos Mills. In the words of C. W. Buchholtz in *Rocky Mountain National Park – A History,* "While many other individuals contributed to the success of the national park, Enos Mills adopted the issue as a personal quest."

The area now occupied by the park had been exploited ever since Joel Estes and his family settled in Estes Park in 1860.

The dedication of Rocky Mountain National Park was held in Horseshoe Park. Looking west up Fall River is Mount Chapin to the right. (Estes Park Museum EP901)

This is another view of the dedication of Rocky Mountain National Park September 4, 1915 in Horseshoe Park. (Colorado Historical Society, Fred Payne Clatworthy)

Herbert N. Wheeler rangers were added to patrol the reserve.

In 1906, the Estes Park Protective and Improvement Association was formed by business leaders to promote the preservation of the area's nature environment. Freelan Stanley and Cornelius Bond took dominant roles, knowing that the future success of Estes Park depended on the area's natural beauty.

While Wheeler stuck to the doctrine of multiple use of the land, including grazing and logging, the ideas of Enos Mills were diametrically opposed to those practices. Mills' vision was the preservation of a vast 1,000-square-mile area free from commercial exploitation, and his views were backed by the protective association. He lobbied to gain the support of prominent business leaders and politicians. Maps were produced to define the area, and in 1913, Robert Marshall of the United States Geological Survey evaluated the area for its scenery and unique geology. He recommended setting aside an area of 700 square miles for a national park.

Mills bombarded the media with over 60 articles, wrote more than 2,000 letters and gave numerous lectures on the subject of establishing a national park. He used his ability as a photographer to illustrate what would be preserved, and argued that the people wanted wilderness.

As mentioned previously, wild game was harvested for Denver restaurants and ranching was the main activity during the early years. With sawmills at Moraine Park, Hollowell Park, Bierstadt Lake and Hidden Valley, an active lumber industry cleared away many of the trees. Rental cabins and lodges sprang up as ranchers found it easier to make a living in the tourist business.

The future site of Rocky Mountain National Park was included within the Medicine Bow Forest Reserve. At first, there was little enforcement of permits required for grazing and logging. Later, under the direction of

Horseshoe Park was filled with a crowd estimated at 2,000 on the dedication day of Rocky Mountain National Park, September 4, 1915.
(Rocky Mountain National Park, Fred Payne Clatworthy 1755)

In 1913, Congress was presented with its first park bill. There were many conflicts over private property, prior logging and grazing permits, water appropriations, and other uses of the land. These issues delayed any action. In June 1914, Congressman Edward Taylor guided the third and final bill through the House of Representatives; Senator Charles Thomas eased it through the Senate. Colorado let our country's leaders know where it stood by sending its big guns to Washington DC – former Governor John Shafroth, retiring Governor Elias Ammons and present Governor-elect George Carlson. Enos Mills was also on hand. On January 26, 1915, President Woodrow Wilson signed Rocky Mountain National Park into law, but it was only a third of the size envisioned by Mills. Size did not matter to the *Denver Post*, which credited Mills as being "The Father of Rocky Mountain National Park."

September 4, 1915 was a milestone in the history of Larimer County as an estimated crowd of 2,000 gathered in Horseshoe Park near what is today's Lawn Lake trailhead. Enthusiasts arrived in horse-drawn wagons and in nearly 300 automobiles. The prestige of having a national park in its backyard had a profound effect on the growth of Estes Park, and marked in increase in tourism all along the Front Range, especially for the towns of Lyons, Longmont and Loveland.

The only one not wearing a hat, Enos Mills seems relaxed at the opening of Rocky Mountain National Park. Next to Mills, holding out an American flag, is Freelan Stanley. On the far right is Colorado Governor George Carlson. (Rocky Mountain National Park)

CHAPTER SEVEN

ROADS

There would have been little hope for Estes Park as a tourist center without good roads and transportation companies. A number of prominent citizens were involved in building this necessary infrastructure.

North St. Vrain

During the 1870s, the Colorado Territorial Legislature encouraged the private investment in toll roads and was willing to grant a decade-long franchise to collect tolls to recoup the investment. Black Canyon rancher Alexander MacGregor envisioned Estes Park as a tourist attraction, but only if good roads were constructed so he filed articles of incorporation for the Park Road Company.

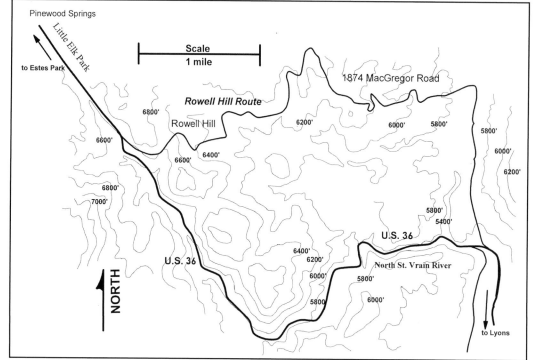

The original stage road to Estes Park followed the North St. Vrain River a short distance before ascending Rowell Hill. This route avoided narrow sections in the North St. Vrain Canyon. (Map drawn by Kenneth Jessen)

Rancher Alexander MacGregor improved the original primitive road up the North St. Vrain River in 1875, as seen in this construction photograph. MacGregor operated it as a toll road, but eventually sold the road to Longmont investors in 1884. (Estes Park Museum EP400)

In 1907, the North St. Vrain route was completely rebuilt using a combination of state and private funds. The road was widened from a single lane to a breadth of at least 14 feet to allow two-way traffic. (Estes Park Museum EP403)

This is the tollgate on the North St. Vrain Road. After the original tollgate was torn down by irate travelers, it was moved to a narrow section of canyon along the Little Thompson River. (Estes Park Museum EP463)

Somewhat similar to the trail pioneered by Joel Estes, MacGregor's route went over the foothills to Little Elk Park, then up Muggins Gulch. He amended his charter with a route that generally followed the North St. Vrain River, but avoided the narrow portion of the canyon by using Rowell Hill to enter Little Elk Park. The MacGregor road entered the Estes Park valley along the base of Mount Olympus through Crocker Ranch and across a vast open area to Black Canyon and MacGregor Ranch.

After its completion in July 1875, MacGregor had trouble maintaining the road. Irate users resented paying a toll and tore down the tollgate where the road entered the foothills. This prompted MacGregor to move the tollgate to a bridge over the Little Thompson River, leaving users little choice but to either ford a deep channel with cold, fast flowing water or pay the toll. By 1882, the road was in such poor condition that the collection of tolls was suspended. In 1884, MacGregor sold the road to Longmont investors.

Roads

This 1908 photograph of Stanley Steamers in the North St. Vrain Canyon shows how close the road was to the stream. The road's location made it easy to refill the water tanks in the steamers. (Estes Park Museum)

Stanley Steamers are lined up at the Lyons depot to take tourists up the North St. Vrain canyon to Estes Park. This view is looking west. (Estes Park Museum)

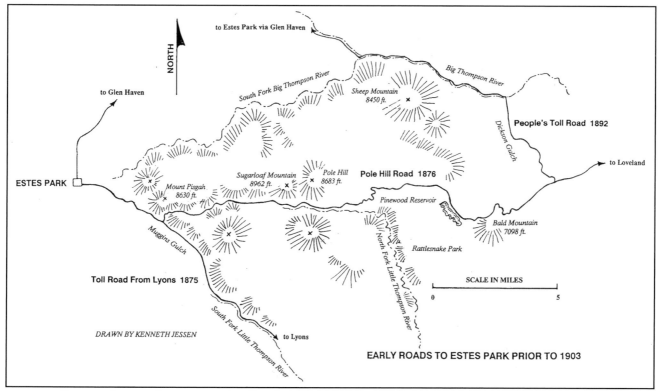

to Estes Park via Glen Haven

NORTH

to Glen Haven

South Fork Big Thompson River

Big Thompson River

Sheep Mountain
8450 ft.

People's Toll Road 1892

Dickson Gulch

to Loveland

ESTES PARK

Mount Pisgah
8630 ft.

Sugarloaf Mountain
8962 ft.

Pole Hill
8683 ft.

Pole Hill Road 1876

Pinewood Reservoir

Bald Mountain
7098 ft.

Muggins Gulch

North Fork Little Thompson River

Rattlesnake Park

SCALE IN MILES

0   5

Toll Road From Lyons 1875

DRAWN BY KENNETH JESSEN

South Fork Little Thompson River

to Lyons

EARLY ROADS TO ESTES PARK PRIOR TO 1903

These are the principle pioneer roads to Estes Park prior to the construction of the road up the Big Thompson Canyon.
The Pole Hill route runs across the center of the map. (Drawing by Kenneth Jessen)

Pole Hill

In 1875, a petition was signed by two dozen Loveland businessmen and presented to the Larimer County Commissioners, proposing to extend an existing road from Bald Mountain over Pole Hill to Estes Park. The commissioners approved the expenditure of approximately $300 to construct the road, but the amount fell far short of what was needed in this rugged country. Nonetheless, through private subscriptions and donated labor, the road was built.

Cliff Cottage, located west of Loveland on Carter Lake Road, stands as a monument to its builder, Zachary Taylor. Constructed in 1885, it once housed the Winona post office and served as a stage stop along the Loveland-Estes Park Pole Hill route.
(Kenneth Jessen)

Pole Hill Road went through Rattlesnake Park (site of Pinewood Reservoir) to Quillan Gulch and climbed up a shallow divide to the North Fork of the Little Thompson River. The road followed the river to Solitude Creek and climbed up Pole Hill. From there, it descended steeply to the existing MacGregor road that continued over Park Hill. Stagecoach service operated by Abner Sprague and his brother used this route between Loveland and Estes Park from 1888 to 1890 with Cliff Cottage as one of the stops (along the present-day Carter Lake Road). In recent years, the remains of what could have been a stage station were discovered near Diamond Spring at the top of the climb to the Little Thompson River. Pole Hill was the first direct route from Loveland to Estes Park, but due to its steep grades and irregular terrain, was never practical.

Big Thompson Canyon

A direct route to Estes Park from Loveland was proposed by a group of Loveland businessmen, to shift some of the tourist trade away from Boulder County to Larimer County. The People's Toll Road, Mining and Manufacturing Company was organized with hopes of making Loveland the undisputed gateway to the Rockies. The charter for this company extended beyond Estes Park and allowed it to build over the Continental Divide into North Park.

To avoid construction difficulties in what was referred to as "The Narrows" in the Big Thompson Canyon, the People's Toll Road followed the first portion of Pole Hill Road up Dry Creek. At the top of the first hill, the road angled up an unnamed gulch to the northwest, then dropped down Dickson Gulch where it joined the canyon at Cedar Cove. The descent down Dickson Gulch was extremely steep, making travel hazardous. From there, the route followed an existing road to Drake. It continued up the North Fork through Knappville (now Glen Haven) to Estes Park. It should be noted that from Drake to Knappville, there were several major deviations from today's road, used to avoid narrow portions of the canyon below Knappville and the steep switchbacks at the head of Devil's Gulch.

The road through "The Narrows" of the Big Thompson was completed in 1904 and provided the first direct water-level route from Loveland to Estes Park. This early view illustrates that the road was one lane wide. (U.S. Geological Survey lwt01275)

The road up the Big Thompson Canyon remained a primitive trail until improvements were made in 1919-1920. Note how close the road is to the river. Springtime flooding often prevented travel. (Loveland Museum/Gallery, Fred Payne Clatworthy)

Abner Sprague took this dramatic, behind-the-wheel photograph in the narrowest section of the Big Thompson Canyon. Turnouts for oncoming traffic were few and far between. (Rocky Mountain National Park)

Stage operators from Loveland to Estes Park included the team of George Foote and Virgil Stoddard, whose livery business in Loveland dates to 1881. Foote already operated a mail route from Greeley to Namaqua west of Loveland, and when the tourist trade began to take shape, Estes Park was added to the route.

Cornelius H. Bond, one of Estes Park Town Company founders and at the time, Larimer County Sheriff, circulated a petition suggesting the construction of a public road up the Big Thompson Canyon following the river through "The Narrows." This water-level route avoided steep grades associated with other routes, but required extensive blasting to establish a roadbed along the near perpendicular canyon walls. The proposed road joined the existing road at Dickson Gulch. At the fork in Drake, the new road went up the South Fork instead of the North Fork, avoiding many of the problems associated with the North Fork route. The petition for the People's Toll Road was successful, and the Larimer County Commissioners solicited bids in 1903.

That June, William A. Riley won the contract at $27,000, but the commissioners only had $24,000 in the treasury. Amid a great deal of public scrutiny, Riley was authorized to begin work and was given a year to complete the project. The schedule was an aggressive one, considering the magnitude of the job. Not only was the roadbed expensive to establish, but a number of bridges had to be installed.

To the amazement of many, in June 1904, Riley declared the road up the Big Thompson Canyon complete. The Larimer County commissioners were apparently still short the full amount of the contract and made claims that the work had not been executed properly. The matter was settled in court and Riley collected most of what was owed to him by Larimer County.

The man standing on the road through "The Narrows" illustrates how perilously close it was to the Big Thompson River. (City of Greeley Museums)

The character of the road up the Big Thompson Canyon can be seen in this photograph taken in the 1920s. By this time, dirt covered the original coarse gravel surface and the road had been widened. (Rocky Mountain National Park)

This part log and part milled lumber bridge across the Big Thompson River was eventually replaced with a reinforced concrete bridge.
(Rocky Mountain National Park)

Although historically important, the pioneer Riley Road up the Big Thompson Canyon would qualify today as nothing more than a primitive four-wheel drive trail. It was dirt with a coarse crushed rock surface and soon became filled with potholes. Because passing turnouts were infrequent, travelers were forced to back up long distances when meeting oncoming traffic. The road was only a few feet above water level and was submerged during the spring runoff.

The road up the Big Thompson Canyon went through a series of major improvements starting in 1908, followed by widening in 1919–1920. In the 1930s, the road was completely reconstructed to become what is now U.S. 34, completed and paved by 1937. This road lasted until 1976 when much of it was destroyed in the Big Thompson Flood. Reconstruction after the flood was an opportunity for further improvements; upgrades which motorists enjoy today.

North St. Vrain Improvements

The new water-level route up the Big Thompson Canyon threatened Longmont and Lyons with the loss of their monopoly on the tourist transportation business. Freelan Stanley easily raised the funds to build new bridges and grade the North St. Vrain route, and he hoped Boulder County would take over its maintenance.

The road still had steep grades over Rowell Hill, which caused a number of accidents. In 1907, Stanley hired John Hall and his son to survey a more satisfactory route. Hall's reports indicated that between the Little Thompson and Lyons, the canyon was so narrow that a great deal of blasting would be required to widen the road, and 60 new bridges were needed. Stanley turned to civil engineer Abner Sprague to survey the same route. This second survey avoided most of the narrow portions of the canyon.

Under Hall's supervision, the new road was built using a combination of state and private funds. Its width was expanded to at least 14 feet to allow two-way traffic, and small concrete dams were built to provide a source of water for Stanley Steamers. The road followed the North St. Vrain for several miles, then made a long cut across the south side of Rowell Hill above the canyon floor. A great deal of this grade is used by present-day U.S. 36, and in places, the original road is visible.

This photograph, taken in the Big Thompson Canyon, illustrates the primitive but scenic nature of the road.
(Library of Congress, Fred Payne Clatworthy)

CHAPTER EIGHT

TRANSPORTATION COMPANIES

Transportation companies were the life-blood of the tourist business in Estes Park. The earliest tourists arrived on rented horseback; later they traveled by horse-drawn wagons and stagecoaches. Stanley Steamers proved equal to the job and for a time, dominated travel. Eventually vehicles with an internal combustion engine, especially from the White Motor Company, replaced the steamers.

Fred Sprague, 1888

Stagecoach service operated by Abner Sprague and his brother Fred used the Pole Hill route between Loveland and Estes Park from 1888 to 1890 with Cliff Cottage as one of the stops (along the present-day Carter Lake Road). Travel was quite difficult due to steep grades, but this road offered the first direct route from Loveland to Estes Park.

In this fine view of Stanley Steamers at the Osborn garage, the vehicles are ready to take guests up the Big Thompson Canyon to Estes Park. (Loveland Museum/Gallery)

This photograph shows Fred Sprague's horse-drawn wagon bringing tourists to his brother's hotel in Moraine Park.
(Rocky Mountain National Park)

Loveland-Estes Park Automobile Company, 1907

Loveland's David O. Osborn and his three sons founded the Loveland-Estes Park Automobile Company in 1907, thus becoming the first to use automobiles between the foothills and Estes Park. The George and Ben Johnson stage line retired the same year to avoid competing with the Osborn men. Osborn's company started with a trio of five-passenger Model F Stanley Steamers and later added nine-passenger vehicles, bringing the company's carrying capacity to 100 passengers a day.

The charge was $3.50 for a one-way trip and $6 for a round trip. The running time to Estes Park in a horse-drawn carriage was 6 1/2 hours in contrast to 3 hours or less in a Stanley Steamer. During his first summer of operation, Osborn took an estimated 3,000 people to the park. A tent on the north side of Elkhorn Avenue served as temporary quarters in Estes Park. It was replaced by a frame garage and ticket office, and in 1915, this structure yielded to a concrete brick building. The following year, the company was sold to Roe Emery's Rocky Mountain Parks Transportation Company.

In anticipation of a lively tourist trade in the canyon, Frank Bartholf built the Forks Hotel at Drake in 1902. The road up the canyon was opened two years later. (Loveland Museum/Gallery)

*David O. Osborn operated the Loveland-Estes Park Automobile Company using the route up the
Big Thompson Canyon. Stanley Steamers were housed in this garage on West Fourth Street in Loveland.
(Loveland Museum/Gallery)*

The morning trip from Loveland stopped at the Forks Hotel at Drake so passengers
could eat lunch while the water tanks in the Stanley Steamers could be refilled. Beyond
Drake, the grade increased to the point where early gasoline-powered vehicles stalled.
The low-end torque of the Steamer easily climbed this grade. The Big Thompson flood
in 1976 destroyed what remained of this portion of the old road.

Estes Park Transportation Company, 1908

To take advantage of the newly reconstructed North St. Vrain road, Freelan Stanley formed the Estes Park Transportation Company in 1908. Centrally located in Estes Park, the depot was constructed that same summer and was set back from Elkhorn Avenue. The building could hold 22 automobiles and was expanded in several stages. In 1915, a new covered section was added; on either side of its entrance were small gable structures, one serving as the freight office and the other as the passenger ticket office. The depot was one lot east of the southeast corner of Elkhorn and Moraine Avenues.

The morning trip from Denver left at 8:20 a.m. and arrived in Estes Park at 1:00 p.m. From the Colorado & Southern depot in Longmont, the fare was $7.50 with 60 cents donated to Boulder County for road improvements. This was the most profitable enterprise Stanley owned in Colorado.

In 1912, Stanley financed a new road from Peaceful Valley to Allenspark, allowing tourists to travel from the railroad depot at Ward to the park. Covering this route was the Ward-Estes Park Auto Line.

Freelan Stanley invested in improving the North St. Vrain road and also founded the Estes Park Transportation Company with its offices in downtown Estes Park. The location was on the south side of Elkhorn Avenue one block east of Moraine Avenue. (Rocky Mountain National Park)

This is a contemporary photograph of a Stanley Steamer mountain wagon with capacity for
11 passengers plus the driver. In the early 1900s, this vehicle dominated transportation to Estes Park
until superseded by the White Motor Company's version of the same basic design.
(Kenneth Jessen)

Denver photographer Louis Charles McClure
ventured over the Ward-to-Estes Park road. This
was the forerunner of the Peak-to-Peak highway
and provided yet another way to reach Estes Park.
In 1912, the Peaceful Valley-to-Allenspark segment
was paid for by Freelan Stanley.
(Library of Congress)

Stanley Steamers are lined up at the Colorado & Southern Loveland depot for the trip to Estes Park through the Big Thompson Canyon.
(Loveland Museum/Gallery)

Rocky Mountain Parks Transportation Company, 1916

Roe Emery built an entire empire on mountain transportation and lodging. In 1914, he had the transportation concession in Glacier National Park and developed a good reputation for low fares and reliable service. In 1916, he purchased Freelan Stanley's Estes Park Transportation Company and formed the Rocky Mountain Parks Transportation Company. This conglomerate also included David O. Osborn's Loveland-Estes Park Automobile Company, Grant Glover's Fort Collins Estes Park Transportation Company, and even Yellow Cab in Denver. In 1919, he became the sole concessionaire for Rocky Mountain National Park. Starting with 26 vehicles, his assets in vehicles grew to 326 vehicles by 1928. He had garages, baggage rooms and ticket offices in Estes Park, Denver, Lyons and Loveland.

In 1919, Emery constructed a large addition behind Stanley's original 1908 building for use as a repair facility and garage. The floor of this structure spanned Fall River. Both of Stanley's structures and Emery's new building would later become the Park Theater Mall, destroyed by fire in October 2009.

Eventually almost all of the Stanley Steamers were replaced by touring cars from the White Motor Company. These automobiles, which commonly traveled in caravans, are easily identifiable in early photographs by the number on the vehicle's hood. Fred Payne Clatworthy would post himself at the large snow drift below Fall River Pass and take photographs of the tourists perched in these touring cars for sale later in the day.

Although there were attempts to monopolize transportation to and from Estes Park, many of the lodges, such as the Lester Hotel, operated their own Stanley Steamers. Shown above is Reverend Charles M. Tresner, one of the hotel drivers. (Charlene Tresner collection)

A caravan of Roe Emery's White Motor Company open touring cars passes through the drift below Fall River Pass with a stop for photographer Fred Payne Clatworthy. In 1919, Emery's Rocky Mountain Parks Transportation Company had a monopoly on commercial operations within the park. (Rocky Mountain National Park, Fred Payne Clatworthy)

Emery's idea was to provide a complete experience for tourist so he offered packages that included scenic trips, meals and lodging. In Estes Park, he purchased the Stanley Hotel and the Lewiston Chalets at Marys Lake, which he renamed the Estes Park Chalets. He also owned the Grand Lake Lodge, and in Clear Creek Canyon, Emery owned the Hot Springs Hotel and the Placer Inn. A typical multi-day trip started in Denver, toured Rocky Mountain National Park, went over to Grand Lake and returned to Denver via Berthoud Pass. With this pre-planned adventure to offer his guests, Emery was able to promote his own facilities for meals and overnight accommodations while also providing the transportation in an all-inclusive package.

The front of the Rocky Mountain Parks Transportation Company can be seen facing Elkhorn Avenue with the freight office on the left and the ticket office on the right. This later became the Park Theater Mall, destroyed by fire in October 2009. (Rocky Mountain National Park)

BIBLIOGRAPHY

PRIMARY SOURCES – BOOKS

Bird, Isabella L. *A Lady's Life in the Rocky Mountains.*
Norman, Oklahoma: University of Oklahoma Press, 1960.

Buchholtz, C. W. *Rocky Mountain National Park, A History.* Boulder:
Colorado Associated University Press, 1983.

Davis, Susan S. *A History and Tour of The Stanley Hotel,
Estes Park, Colorado.* Estes Park: The Stanley Museum, 1999.

Early Estes Park Narratives, Volume I, Discovery, Settlement, and
Recreation. Pickering, James H. (editor). Estes Park: Alpenaire
Publishing Inc. in cooperation with the Estes Park Museum, 2004.

Gates, Zethyl and Ann Hilfinger. *Historical Images from the
Loveland Museum/Gallery Collection.* Loveland, Colorado:
Loveland Museum/Gallery, 1994.

Mills, Enos A. *Early Estes Park, Rocky Mountain National Park and
Grand Lake.* Estes Park, Colorado: Enos Mills Cabin,
1905 (original copyright).

Pickering, James H., Carey Stevanus and Mic Clinger. *Estes Park and
Rocky Mountain National Park Then & Now.* Evergreen,
Colorado: Westcliffe Publishers, 2006.

Pickering, James H. *Mr. Stanley of Estes Park.* Kingfield, Maine: Stanley
Museum, 2000.

Pickering, James H. *This Blue Hollow.* Niwot, Colorado:
University Press of Colorado, 1999.

Pickering, James H. *America's Switzerland.* Boulder, Colorado:
University Press of Colorado, 2005.

Pickering, James H. *The MacGregors of Black Canyon: An
American Story.* Estes Park, Colorado: Muriel L. MacGregor
Trust, 2008.

Pederson, Henry F. Jr. *Those Castles of Wood.* Self-published, 1993.

PRIMARY SOURCES – NEWSPAPER ARTICLES

"Addition to Garage Adds Convenience," *Estes Park Alikasai,*
April 23, 1915.

"Brown Tea Pot being Rebuilt," *Estes Park Alikasai,* April 23, 1915.

Bush, Mel. "Elkhorn Lodge Founded in 1877," *Estes Park Trail Gazette,*
April 2, 1984.

Bibliography

"C. F. Boettcher and his wife have gone to Estes Park,"
Loveland Reporter, February 13, 1908.

"Canyon Road in Excellent Condition," *Loveland Reporter*,
January 9, 1908.

"Dunraven Holdings Bought" *Denver Republican*, April 4, 1903.

"Dutch Kitchen will be Known as Prospect Inn," *Estes Park Alikasai*,
April 23, 1915.

"Great Improvements in Estes Park," *Estes Park Alikasai*,
April 23, 1915.

Hondius, Elenor E. "Elkhorn Lodge," unpublished manuscript,
Estes Park Public Library.

"Jim Nugent Dies" *Rocky Mountain News*, September 15, 1874.

"Lewiston New Hotel Under Construction," *Estes Park
Alikasai*, April 23, 1915.

"Manford House Open," *The Mountaineer*, June 11, 1908,
Volume 1, No. 2.

"Mountain Jim" *Rocky Mountain News*, July 24, 1874.

"New Bank Organized in Estes Park," *Loveland Reporter*,
February 27, 1908.

"New Garage for Automobile Line is being Built," *Estes Park Alikasai*,
April 23, 1915.

"New Stanley Hotel - Not to be called The Dunraven but what it will
be called, yet to be decided," *The Mountaineer*, August 27, 1908,
Volume 1, No. 13.

"Sold for a Yoke of Oxen" *Rocky Mountain News*, September 15, 1874.

"Some of the things in Estes Park," *The Mountaineer*, July 9, 1908.

Sprague, Abner E. "The Estes and Rocky Mountain National Parks,"
Estes Park Trail, April 27, 1923.

Tomlinson, John. Letter to the editor. *Denver Republican*.
July 10, 1902.

BOOKLETS

A Pictorial History of Estes Park, Colorado. Roger Bergquist, editor.
Self-published, 1968.

Bancroft, Caroline. *Estes Park and Trail Ridge*. Boulder:
Johnson Publishing Company, 1967.

Stauffer, Ruth. *This was Estes Park*. Estes Park, Colorado:
Estes Park Area Historical Museum, 1976
(Revised edition 1990).

Benedict, Diane Goode. *Birth of a Quarry Town 1800s Lyons,
Colorado*. Lyons, Colorado: Applications Press, 2002.

Canning, Anne Smedley. *Early Estes Park*. Self-published, 1990.

Carothers, June E. *Estes Park, Past and Present*. Denver:
University of Denver Press, 1951.

Cassell, Colleen Estes. *The Golden Pioneer - Biography of Joel Estes*.
Seattle: Peanut Butter Publishing, 1999.

Columbian Industrial Edition, 1894, *Fort Collins Express*.

BOOKS

Dunning, Harold Marion. *Over Hill and Vale*. Boulder,
Colorado: Johnson Publishing Company, 1956.

Dunning, Harold Marion. *Over Hill and Vale, Volume II.* Boulder, Colorado: Johnson Publishing Company, 1962.

Dunning, Harold Marion. *Over Hill and Vale, Volume III.* Boulder, Colorado: Johnson Publishing Company, 1962.

Dunning, Harold Marion. *The History of Estes Park.* Boulder: Johnson Publishing Company, 1967.

Dunning, Harold Marion. *Facts About Longs Peak.* Boulder: Johnson Publishing Company, 1970.

Drummond, Alexander. *Enos Mills, Citizen of Nature.* Niwot, Colorado: University Press of Colorado, 1995.

Early Estes Park Narratives, Volume II, Discovery, Settlement, and Recreation. Pickering, James H. (editor). Estes Park: Alpenaire Publishing Inc. in cooperation with the Estes Park Museum, 2004.

Early Estes Park Narratives, Volume III, Days and Hours of Estes Park (1912-1944). Pickering, James H. (editor). Estes Park: Alpenaire Publishing Inc. in cooperation with the Estes Park Museum, 2004.

Early Estes Park Narratives, Volume IV, Narratives of Exploration and Mountain Adventure. Pickering, James H. (editor). Estes Park: Alpenaire Publishing Inc. in cooperation with the Estes Park Museum, 2004.

Foscue, Edwin J. and Louis O. Quam. *Estes Park, Resort in the Rockies.* Dallas: University Press in Dallas, 1949.

Frederick Chapin's Colorado. Pickering, James H. (editor). Niwot, Colorado: University Press of Colorado, 1995.

Freudenburg, Betty D. et. al. Facing the Frontier, *The Story of the MacGregor Ranch.* Estes Park: The Rocky Mountain Nature Association, 1998.

Hicks, Dave. *Estes Park, From The Beginning.* Self-published, 1976.

Kaye, Evelyn. *Amazing Traveler Isabella Bird.* Boulder: Blue Penguin Publications, 1994.

Loveland-Big Thompson Valley 1877 Centennial 1977. Ball, Clara (editor). Loveland, Colorado: Loveland-Big Thompson Valley Centennial Commission Inc., 1975.

Melton, Jack R. and Lulabeth Melton. YMCA of the Rockies - Reflections, *Traditions and Visions.* Estes Park, Colorado: YMCA of the Rockies, 2006.

Melton, Jack R. and Lulabeth Melton. *YMCA of the Rockies - Spanning a Century.* Estes Park, Colorado: YMCA of the Rockies, 1992.

Pickering, James H. *Enos Mills' Colorado.* Boulder: Johnson Books, 2006.

Osterwald, Doris B. *Rocky Mountain Splender.* Lakewood: Western Guideways Inc., 1989

Posser, Glenn. *The Saga of Black Canyon.* Self-published, 1971.

Sprague, Abner E. *My Pioneer Life, The Memoirs of Abner E. Sprague.* Estes Park: Rocky Mountain Nature Association, 1999.

Stansfield, John. *Enos Mills - Rocky Mountain Naturalist.* Palmer Lake, Colorado: Filter Press, 2005.

Watrous, Ansel. *History of Larimer County, Colorado.* Fort Collins, Colorado: The Courier Printing & Publishing Company, 1911.

INDEX

Passengers in a car from Kansas get their first view of the Estes Park Valley from Park Hill.
This same view is enjoyed today by those traveling on U.S. 36.
(Rocky Mountain National Park)